Railways & Recollections 1978

Contents

Introduction	2
January	4
February	9
March	13
April	19
May	22
June	29
July	32
August	34
September	36
October	38
November	41
December	43
1978 Happenings	4, 12, 18, 27, 44
1978 Arrivals & Departures	14
No 1 Records	47
Index	48

© David Phillips 2015
Photographs © The NOSTALGIA Collection archive

All rights reserved. No part of this publication may be reproduced, stored in a retrieval system or transmitted, in any form or by any means, electronic, mechanical, photocopying, recording or otherwise, without prior permission in writing from Silver Link Publishing Ltd.

First published in 2015

British Library Cataloguing in Publication Data

A catalogue record for this book is available from the British Library.

ISBN 978 1 85794 404 4

Silver Link Publishing Ltd
The Trundle
Ringstead Road
Great Addington
Kettering
Northants NN14 4BW

Tel/Fax: 01536 330588
email: sales@nostalgiacollection.com
Website: www.nostalgiacollection.com

Printed and bound in the Czech Republic

Frontispiece: **ARMATHWAITE** Steam traction had ended ten years earlier, but it was very much a case of 'gone but not forgotten'. At first British Rail had banned steam engines from its rails, but by 1978 had relented and special steam-hauled rail tours like this 'Norfolkman' tour on the Settle-Carlisle line on 25 March 1978 were hugely popular. The Gresley-designed *Green Arrow* is far from its old Eastern Region haunts, but LNER No 4771 was the sort of powerful locomotive needed to take on the challenges of the famous trans-Pennine route. In this picture, *Green Arrow*'s restorer, Bill Harvey, is being presented with various awards for all his hard work in getting the locomotive back in working order.

Introduction

1978 was a year of transition for Britain and its railways. It was a time when the country was being torn apart by industrial strife on a scale never seen before. It was ridiculed as 'the sick man of Europe' – a situation not helped by a weak minority Labour Government, propped up by half-hearted Liberal support in the so-called Lib-Lab Pact, and afraid to confront the unions. Meanwhile, a certain Margaret Thatcher was waiting in the wings, as leader of the Conservative opposition.

Steam power had ended on British railways a decade earlier, but much of the Victorian infrastructure remained. British Rail's engineers and managers had plenty of energy and imaginative ideas for the future, but the nationalised rail industry was starved of investment by a cash-strapped Government.

The rolling stock was a mixed lot. The modernisation of the system in the 1950s and '60s had seen a bewildering variety of diesel motive power introduced to replace the steam fleet. Some were successful, others frankly poor – but most still limped on in service in 1978.

True, powerful Intercity 125s were now roaring down the main lines at 125mph. But on less prestigious lines, trains were more likely to be hauled by an asthmatic diesel-burner that would struggle to pull the skin off a rice pudding!

Even on the main lines, passenger accommodation was often well past its sell-by date. It was a national joke, only it wasn't at all funny on 6 July 1978 when a fire broke out in an elderly sleeping car in the Penzance-Paddington express. The BR Mark 1 car (No W2437) had been built in 1960, when coaches relied upon steam engines for their heating. After steam was axed, some diesel locomotives were fitted with boilers to provide heating, but it was an unsatisfactory arrangement and most coaches were converted to electric heating, with a self-contained electric heater in the vestibule.

Unfortunately, on the fateful night in question somebody had left a polythene sack full of dirty linen in the vestibule of sleeping car No W2437, propped against the heater. It first smouldered, then burst into flames. By the time the fire was discovered, near Taunton, 11 people had already died, mainly from carbon monoxide poisoning. A 12th died later, in hospital, and 15 others were injured.

The Taunton fire occurred just as new Mark 3 sleeping cars were at the design stage, and the old Mark 1 vehicles were phased out by the early 1980s. Happily, the Mark 3s have an excellent safety record.

On a brighter note, travellers on the West Coast Main Line in 1978 could see the new town of Milton Keynes getting bigger by the day. The town's controversial concrete cows, installed in a field by the railway this year, no doubt made many a passenger chuckle.

This was also the year that motorcycle manufacturer Norton Villiers Triumph went into liquidation. Just two decades earlier, Britain had led the world in two-wheeler production. Now, like so many of the UK's industry, it was rapidly becoming moribund. Unemployment reached a post-war high of 1.5 million in 1978.

Amid all the doom and gloom, escapism was welcome. Some folk found it in pop music, and the upbeat harmonies of Boney M saw the group score three No 1 hit singles during the year. But others preferred to climb aboard a train and explore Britain by watching the scenery unfold beyond their carriage window.

Ray Ruffell, who took the superb photographs in this book, certainly did just that. A railwayman by both profession and inclination, he took his camera with him everywhere he went. Although his working career was based in the Southern Region, his holidays took him to every corner of the country's rail network – as you will see. Ray's camerawork is a priceless glimpse into a fast-changing Britain. Inside you'll see huge, locomotive-hauled coal trains serving the country's massive collieries and industrial complexes, as well as stunning rural landscapes unchanged since the lines were built by the Victorian rail pioneers.

Little did he know at the time that he was recording a landscape that would all too soon change for ever. In 1979 the Conservatives would sweep to power and their leader, Margaret Thatcher, was bristling for a fight with the unions. Within a decade, the mining and heavy manufacturing industries were a shadow of their former selves.

Mrs Thatcher was no fan of the railways, which she also associated with awkward union leaders and strike-happy workers. There would be no rail renaissance on her watch. In retrospect, it is clear that 1978 was very much the end of an era. We should all be grateful to Ray for recording that final pre-Thatcher year so comprehensively.

If you want to see what Britain was really like back then, you'll be fascinated as 1978 unfolds, month by month. Ray didn't just snap the big, glamorous express trains. He loved the grimy industrial shunters and gritty urban landscapes every bit as much as the shiny and new, as you'll see as you turn these pages – and enjoy!

1978 Happenings

January
- A North Sea storm causes widespread flooding and destroys piers at Hunstanton, Skegness, Herne Bay and Margate.

- Three-month firefighters' strike ends when fire crews accept an offer of a 10% pay rise.

- 18-year-old prostitute Helen Rytka is murdered in Huddersfield – the eighth victim of the 'Yorkshire Ripper'.

February
- Leeds United defender Gordon McQueen becomes Britain's first £500,000 player when he is sold to Manchester United.

- Anna Ford becomes Britain's first female newsreader on ITN.

- Opinion polls show the Conservative opposition 11 points ahead of Labour Government.

LONDON Heathrow Central was the final phase of the Piccadilly Line's extension from Hounslow West to the airport. The preceding station, Hatton Cross, had opened as the interim terminus in 1975.

January

LONDON Heathrow Central tube station had opened on 16 December 1977, but it was three weeks later in early January before Ray got round to paying a visit. The new station served as the terminus of what became known as the Heathrow branch of the Piccadilly Line – previously it had been the Hounslow branch. It was the first time that an airport had been directly served by an underground railway system.

LONDON It is hard to believe that Heathrow Central was so quiet back in 1978! These days it is usually packed with travellers – and it is no longer the airport's only underground station. In 1986 it was renamed Heathrow Central Terminals 1, 2, 3 when Heathrow Terminal 4 station opened to serve the new fourth terminal. Heathrow Terminal 5 station opened in 2008, but the frequency of trains on the Heathrow branch of the Piccadilly Line remained the same.

READING It's 13 January and Ray is on hand with his camera to capture an InterCity 125 rush through Reading station at high speed. In fact, the powerful DMU is the fastest train ever to run on Brunel's famous rails, trimming the timetable from Paddington to Penzance (not to mention Bristol and South Wales) in the process.

Ever since the late 1950s British Railways (later British Rail) had wanted to achieve higher speeds on its main express routes, so that the trains could compete with Britain's new motorways. A team of engineers was assembled in Derby in the early 1960s with the aim of developing an advanced passenger train (APT) capable of at least 125 miles per hour and tilting to allow higher speeds on bends.

But the ambitious APT project had suffered repeated delays, and in 1970 BR bosses authorised the development of a non-tilting high-speed diesel train for short-term use until the APT was able to take over.

The InterCity 125 was built from 1975 to 1982 and was introduced in 1976 on the Western Region. It operated at speeds of up to 125mph in regular service, with a maximum speed of 148mph, making it the fastest diesel-powered train in the world – a record it still holds today.

By the start of the summer timetable in May 1977 the full complement of 27 Class 253 sets (Nos 253001-27) was in service on the Western Region, completely replacing locomotive-hauled trains on the Bristol and South Wales routes. The displacement by HSTs of Class 50 locomotives to slower services effectively finished off the last of the elderly 'Western' Class 52 diesel-hydraulics by early 1977. HST services were extended for most daytime trains from London to Devon and Cornwall. Some South Wales services were extended to Milford Haven, Fishguard and Pembroke in West Wales.

After three decades the majority of the HST fleet is still in service. Most are expected to be replaced within the next 10 years, but a number will continue in use on London to Devon/Cornwall services, where there are no plans to electrify the lines.

Above: **READING**
Pictured on the same day are two of the Class 50 diesels that the HSTs are soon to replace – in this case Nos 50028 and 50030 on an up West of England express.

Right: **READING**
And here is a three-car cross-country DMU about to depart for Paddington.

Above: **HUDDERSFIELD**
Ray made one of his regular forays north on 26 January, where he captured Class 47 No 47501 departing from the distinctive Huddersfield station at the head of the 10.10 Liverpool-Newcastle express.

Right: **HUDDERSFIELD**
The cotton barons of the northern mill towns in Victorian times loved grandiose public buildings – hence the impressive columns at the main entrance to Huddersfield station.

CLAYTON WEST While in West Yorkshire Ray couldn't resist taking this photograph of a National Coal Board 0-4-0 Hudswell shunter in action with mineral trucks at Clayton West. We're glad he did, because the coaling operation has long since disappeared. Clayton West closed five years later, in 1983, but reopened in 1992 as the terminus of the preserved Kirklees Light Railway.

SHEFFIELD Later that day, in Sheffield, Ray spotted Class 45 No 45133 at the head of the 14.10 departure to London St Pancras.

Right: **SURBITON** On 30 January heavy rain caused this embankment slip, causing the up local line to be closed while contractors put it right.

February

Below: **LONDON** Again, Ray starts his month by going underground – this time on 2 February to London's Post Office Railway, which runs for nearly 7 miles beneath the capital, from Paddington in the west to Whitechapel in the east, with seven intermediate stations, each serving major sorting offices above. Here we see the biggest of the lot, Mount Pleasant, which also serves as a depot for the 40mph driverless trains.

Far right: **LONDON** Here's the workshop at Mount Pleasant, with a gang carrier (which as its name suggests is for moving Post Office personnel) in for service.

Below right: **LONDON** Still at Mount Pleasant, the little trains are clearly busy. The idea of building the 2-foot narrow-gauge railway came in 1911, because it took so long to transport mail across the capital by road due to congestion (no change there, then…). Work commenced in 1915, but was postponed in 1917 due to shortage of manpower and materials caused by the First World War. A year later work recommenced and it was completed in 1927.

The system was mothballed in 2013, not because it wasn't effective, but because many of the surface sorting offices had moved location.

The British Postal Museum and Archive has recently announced plans to build a museum and open part of the line to the public, in 2020.

LONDON Later in the day Ray went overground to snap this Circle Line train in the open air at Farringdon Street.

Above: **MANCHESTER** Back up north again on 10 February, Ray spotted Class 40 No 40035 hauling Merseyrail stock through Ashburys station, following wheel turning at Reddish.

Above right: **PORTSMOUTH** Here's another Class 40, this time a superbly turned-out No 40173, this time hauling a 'Whistler' rail tour on 11 February.

Right: **PORTSMOUTH** Here's tour organiser Les Kent posing alongside the mighty loco at Fratton. Class 40s were known as 'Whistlers', on account of the whistling noise made by the 2,000bhp English Electric engine. Some 200 were built between 1947 and 1954, and they were initially used on main-line express links, but the introduction of ever more powerful locos saw them relegated to less glamorous roles and all were withdrawn by 1985.

The most infamous member of the class was No 40126, the locomotive stopped at Sears Crossing on the West Coast Main Line during the 1963 'Great Train Robbery'.

1978 Happenings

March
- *The Hitchhiker's Guide to the Galaxy* is broadcast on Radio 4.

April
- UK's first official naturist beach opens at Fairlight Glen in Covehurst Bay, Sussex.
- Radio broadcasts of proceedings in the House of Commons begin.
- Nottingham Forest win the Football League First Division title for the first time in their history, led by manager Brian Clough.
- Izhar Cohen & the Alphabeta win the Eurovision Song Contest for Israel with their song *A-Ba-Ni-Bi*.

May
- 1 May becomes a UK bank holiday for the first time.
- Ipswich Town win the FA Cup, beating Arsenal 1-0.
- Liverpool retain the European Cup with a 1-0 win over Belgian champions Club Brugge.

LONDON In the middle of February much of Britain was gripped by freezing conditions and heavy snow. On the 20th Class 418 EMU No 1121 has arrived at Waterloo after soldiering on through blizzards and snowdrifts – only to fail when it was needed for its next departure.

LONDON And here it is being towed away by Class 73 No 73108. The Class 73 was an electro-diesel locomotive that could operate either from the Southern Region's 650/750V DC third rail or by means of an on-board diesel engine to allow it to operate on non-electrified routes. This made the class very versatile, although the diesel engine produced less power than was available from the third-rail supply. Forty-nine were built from 1962 to 1967.

March

LONDON On 13 March Ray and his camera were at King's Cross for what railway folk nicknamed 'Juice Inauguration Day', but which was officially the switching on of the long-awaited (and long-winded-sounding) Great Northern Suburban Electrification Project. This allowed suburban EMUs to run between the terminus and Hitchin. Electrification to Peterborough followed in 1987, Doncaster and York in 1989, Newcastle in 1990 and finally, in 1991, Edinburgh.

LONDON Another view of King's Cross, this time with one of the new EMUs about to depart in the foreground and Class 40 No 40077 in the background, awaiting its next duty.

1978 Arrivals & Departures

LONDON With Eastern rails beckoning, Ray couldn't resist hopping on the 09.10 northwards. Here's the view of Finsbury Park diesel depot from his carriage window.

BROUGH Here he is later in the day in Yorkshire, where he photographed the Hull portion of a train from King's Cross about to depart behind Class 31 No 31417.

Arrivals
Alex Leigh	Model	1 January
Janine Machin	Radio presenter	24 February
Samantha Judge	Scottish field hockey forward	22 March
Stephen Clemence	Footballer	31 March
Matthew Goode	Actor	3 April
Rachel Stevens	Singer	9 April
Katie Price	Model	22 May
Carl Barât	Musician (The Libertines)	6 June
Matthew Bellamy	Singer	9 June
Dan Wheldon	Racing driver	22 June
Callum Blue	Actor	19 August
Jodie Kidd	Model	25 September
Rachel McAdams	Actress	17 November
Damien Johnson	Footballer	18 November
Katie Holmes	Actress	18 December
Jodie Marsh	Model	23 December

Departures
Harold Abrahams	Athlete (b1899)	14 January
Herbert Sutcliffe	Cricketer (b1894)	22 January
Paul Scott	Novelist, playwright and poet (b1920)	1 March
Sir Morien Morgan	Aeronautics engineer (b1912)	4 April
Sir Clough Williams-Ellis	Architect (b1883)	9 April
Sandy Denny	Folk singer (b1947)	21 April
Selwyn Lloyd	Politician (b1904)	18 May
John Mackintosh	Politician (b1929)	30 July
Nicolas Bentley	Writer and illustrator (b1907)	14 August
Robert Shaw	Actor (b1927)	28 August
Keith Moon	Drummer (The Who) (b1946)	7 September
Hugh MacDiarmid	Poet (b1892)	9 September
Pope John Paul I	(b1912)	28 September
Nancy Spungen	Girlfriend of Sex Pistol Sid Vicious (b1958)	12 October
Golda Meir	Israeli Prime Minister (b1898)	8 December

BROUGH Metro-Cammell DMUs were staple fare for cross-country services in the East Riding. This is the 12.15 Hull to Goole, about to depart.

KNOTTINGLEY Coal trains at Kellingley Colliery, near Knottingley. When it opened in 1965, this deep coal mine (800 metres) employed about 2,000. It was also one of the last in Yorkshire to survive, but is due to close this year (2015).

BRORA A week later, Ray and his family were in Sutherland, in the Highlands of Scotland, heading to Wick from Inverness. The approaching train is heading in the opposite direction, hauled by Class 26 No 26025.

HELMSDALE The line to the North of Scotland hugs the coastline, as can be seen from Ray's shot through the carriage window.

WICK Arrival at Wick after the long but scenic haul from Inverness.

ACHNASHEEN Later Ray headed for Kyle of Lochalsh from Inverness, on a stopping train hauled by Class 26 No 26044.

STROME FERRY The oil rig construction yard is complete with a Hudswell 0-6-0 diesel shunter. Nearby is one of the best-selling motor cars of the 1970s – the Mark 3 Cortina. It looks like it's the top-of-the-range Ghia spec, with a vinyl roof adding a touch of luxury.

March

KYLE OF LOCHALSH The end of the line – and what a view of the Isle of Skye! Back in 1978, a car and passenger ferry ran from the station to the island, but in 1995 it was replaced by the Skye Bridge.

PERTH Class 26 No 26024 is ready for the journey to Edinburgh – from where Ray and family will head back south again via the ECML.

GARSDALE A crowd gathers to watch ex-LNER No 4771 *Green Arrow* take on water during the 'Norfolkman' rail tour from Leeds to Carlisle on 25 March (see also page 1). This was the only survivor of the 'V2' Class of 2-6-2 mixed-traffic locomotives designed by legendary LNER engineer Sir Nigel Gresley. Between 1936 and 1944 184 'V2s' were built at Darlington and Doncaster. No 4771 was the first to be built and was named after the express freight service for which it had been designed.

DENT Another view of No 4771 during its tour along the Settle-Carlisle line. Arguably England's most scenic main line, it was constructed in the 1870s and is 73 miles long. British Rail wanted to close the line in the 1980s, claiming that it would cost too much to repair its neglected infrastructure – most notably the famous Ribblehead Viaduct – but the public was no longer in the mood for rail closures, having seen the effects of the 1960s Beeching cuts, and massive protests saw BR change its mind. Today, the Settle-Carlisle is busy, makes a profit and is a huge tourist attraction.

1978 Happenings (3)

May (continued)
- 40-year-old prostitute Vera Millward is found stabbed to death in the grounds of the Manchester Royal Infirmary Hospital – the tenth victim of the 'Yorkshire Ripper'.

June
- Freddie Laker is knighted.

- Naomi James becomes the first woman to sail around the world single-handedly.

- Cricketer Ian Botham becomes the first man in the history of the game to score a century and take eight wickets in one innings of a Test match.

- Andrew Lloyd Webber/Tim Rice musical *Evita* opens in London.

- Argentina defeats the Netherlands 3–1 to win the World Cup.

July
- 12 die in Taunton train fire – the worst rail accident since Hither Green in 1967.

- Solomon Islands become independent from the United Kingdom.

April

Right: **READING** On 4 April Class 47 No 47002 heads a train loaded with 'GLC rubbish', as Ray notes on the back of this photograph. Presumably he means domestic waste heading for a landfill site, and not the verbal garbage for which the Greater London Council was so often famous! The GLC was abolished in 1986 by the Local Government Act, which was seen by most political commentators as a punishment doled out by Margaret Thatcher for the excesses of the big metropolitan councils like the GLC under Labour control.

Below: **READING** A busy interlude at Reading station on 7 April, with an InterCity 125 picking up passengers at the up platform, Class 31 No 31280 heading empty newspaper stock bound for London, and EMU No 7385 standing at the down platform.

YORK On 22 April Ray enjoyed a day out at York and its famous rail museum, also photographing an eclectic collection of main-line diesels. Here, nose to nose, are Class 45 No 45030 and an unidentified Class 40.

YORK And here is Class 40 No 40052 and an unidentified Class 37.

YORK Drivers Bernard Tippen and Norman Lawrence are dwarfed by this Class 37.

YORK In the foreground is a member of one of the most famous diesel classes ever built – the 'Deltics' (Class 55) – designed to replace Gresley's legendary 'Pacifics' on the East Coast Main Line in the early 1960s. Twenty-two were built and they remained in service until 1978, when they were replaced by the InterCity 125s. Six were preserved, including one in York's National Railway Museum, which opened in 1975 in the former York North loco depot, close to the station.

April

YORK One of the museum's star attractions was the Advanced Passenger Train APT-3 – a concept train that achieved a new British railway speed record on 10 August 1975 when it hit 152.3mph. Built in 1972 and powered by gas turbines, it was so successful that British Rail went on to build three APT-P prototypes. The ultimate aim was to create tilting trains for speeds of up to 155mph on the twisty West Coast Main Line. Unfortunately, the trains' launch in 1981 was a flop – they were not ready and plagued with problems, and were quietly withdrawn from service soon afterwards.

HOOTON On 29 April Ray was in Cheshire, where he snapped Class 40 No 40185 at Hooton station.

May

BIRKENHEAD On 5 May Ray travelled to the Wirral peninsula. At Rock Ferry he snapped these EMUs; that on the left, with Driving Trailer Open Second No M29131M leading, is about to depart for Liverpool Central.

POOLE The following day, the 6th, Ray is back down south – in Poole, Dorset, where he photographed a train of empty coaching stock passing through the station.

May

Below: **SURBITON** A minor drama on 7 May: Class 74 No E6104, freshly arrived from Southampton, has just failed after leaving Surbiton, and is given a tow by Class 73 No E6007.

No E6104 was originally one of 24 Class 71s built at British Railways' Doncaster Works between 1958 and 1960. Unlike most other Southern Region electric locomotives, they could not operate away from the electrified (750V DC third rail) system. In the late 1960s No E6104 was one of ten converted to run either on electrical supply or by means of an on-board diesel engine, becoming Class 74. All were scrapped by 1981.

Above: **POOLE** On the same day Class 47 No 47557 arrives to form the 17.05 to Liverpool Lime Street.

May

WIMBLEDON On 12 May Ray took a wander around the London Underground depot at Wimbledon. Here is a train of Waterloo & City stock.

WIMBLEDON On the same day Ray's friend, the Rev Charles Pond, poses for the camera before heading back to Tower Hill on the District Line.

Left: **LYMINGTON** Class 423 EMU No 7735 arrives at Lymington Pier on 14 May. It was built at York in 1967-68 and was one of 194 in its class.

Right: **LYMINGTON** They say it's possible to walk across Lymington Harbour, from boat to boat, without getting your feet wet. That certainly appears to be the case in this shot of yachts at anchor, taken through the carriage window.

Above: **LYMINGTON** Another view of unit No 7735. Alternative transport on offer includes a Ford Escort Mark 1 and a Puch moped.

Above right: **READING** Class 33 Nos 33014 and 33012 are at the head of a Stratford-Millbrook Freightliner train on 17 May.

Right: **READING** An InterCity 125 roars along Old Bank as it heads for Paddington.

LONDON HST set No 254008 sits at King's Cross on 20 May, about to depart for Edinburgh forming the most famous service of all – the 'Flying Scotsman'.

1978 Happenings

July (continued)
- Louise Brown becomes the world's first 'test-tube baby'.

August
- US Army Sergeant Walter Robinson 'walks' across the English Channel in 11 hours 30 minutes, using homemade floating shoes.

September
- Bulgarian dissident Georgi Markov is stabbed with a poison-tipped umbrella as he walks across Waterloo Bridge, London.
- 23 Ford car plants are closed across Britain due to strikes.

October
- Government announces the new GCSE exam to replace O Levels and CSEs.
- Ceremony marks the completion of Liverpool Cathedral, the foundation stone of which was laid in 1904.

November
- Dominica gains independence from the United Kingdom.
- British bakeries impose bread rationing after a bakers' strike led to panic buying.

LONDON It's 27 May and Ray is at Liverpool Street, where he photographs this Underground train of C77 stock on the Circle Line.

IPSWICH Ray had been at Liverpool Street to take a train to Suffolk. This is Ipswich station, where a Class 37 is arriving at the head of the 11.42 Norwich to Liverpool Street train, while on the left a Class 31 will soon depart with the 10.52 Liverpool Street to Great Yarmouth service. Note the impressive semaphore signals.

June

SHEFFIELD On 17 June Ray joined the 'Chopper' rail tour through South Yorkshire and the Midlands, hauled by a brace of Class 20s locomotives, which were nicknamed 'Choppers' on account of the distinctive beat that their engines produced when under load, resembling the sound of a helicopter. Some 228 Class 20s were built between 1957 and 1968. They were designed for light mixed-traffic work, with a modest output of just over 1,000bhp. Because of this, many were twin-coupled to deliver a much more useful 2,000bhp.

In this photograph, Nos 20013 and 20170 are barely visible at the front of the train as it skirts the massive Tinsley Marshalling Yard. Opened in 1965 as a part of a major plan to rationalise rail services in the Sheffield area, the yard was closed in stages from 1985 with the run-down of rail freight in Britain. It was also the site of Tinsley Traction Maintenance Depot, which was closed in 1998. At its peak, 200 locomotives were allocated to this depot.

At the time of opening the marshalling yard was handling 3,000 wagons a day. Incoming trains were split in the 11 reception sidings and propelled over the hump, from where the individual wagons or groups of wagons rolled down to form new trains in the 50 main sorting sidings. Tinsley even had its own dedicated class of shunter (Class 13), as BR's standard class of shunting locomotive was not powerful enough for use in the yard.

NOTTINGHAM From Sheffield, the tour headed for Toton, a suburb of Nottingham dominated by Toton Sidings – another huge marshalling yard, from which coal from the Nottinghamshire coalfield was sorted before being sent to the rest of the country. Today the sidings have been earmarked for a station on the proposed HS2 rail link. Among the locos on display in this picture is another 'Chopper', Class 20 No 20180.

Above: **NOTTINGHAM** Here's a HAA hopper of coal in Toton Sidings, probably destined for the nearby Beeston coal-fired power station.

Above right: **STOURBRIDGE** On to the West Midlands now, where the 'Chopper' rail tour halts at Stourbridge Junction for a photo opportunity. Although it looks like the front, this is technically the rear of 'Chopper' No 20013.

STOURBRIDGE Note the melee of enthusiasts congregated around the front of the train. Even in 1978 it was clear that there were plenty of fans for diesel locomotives, just as there had been steam locos before them!

STOURBRIDGE This is how the 'front' ends of the two locomotives are coupled.

WORCESTER Finally here's another view of the special, at the city's Shrub Hill station.

July

AYR Three weeks after the 'Chopper' tour of the English Midlands, Ray travelled to Scotland where he chanced upon another brace of Class 20s – Nos 20200 and 20083 – at work in Ayr Harbour.

AYR And here they are again, a little later, at Killoch Colliery, hauling mineral wagons.

AYR The pair shunt their brake van in the colliery sidings before picking up loaded wagons.

AYR Seen from inside the brake van, guard Dave Monger has a conversation with a fellow Scottish Region guard.

LONDON Back on Southern rails on 21 July, Ray spotted this heavy coal train making slow progress through Clapham Junction.

MARCHWOOD The 'Marchwood Volunteer' rail tour on 22 July left Waterloo for the military port of the same name on the western shore of Southampton Water. There it was headed by ex-War Department 0-6-0 *Waggoner*, coupled to two ex-BR coaches and DEMU Nos 1306 and 1313 – quite a collection!

MARCHWOOD The crowd appear to be ignoring the little industrial loco for something going on in the background. Perhaps something interesting was happening at Marchwood station, which had been closed to passenger traffic since February 1966, although it was still open for freight. Situated between Totton and Hythe, Marchwood nestles on the fringe of the New Forest, but is very much an industrial area.

Left: **HAMBLE** The rail tour later ventured to the far side of Southampton Water, to Hamble, where Ray photographed the DEMUs at the rear of the train. Hamble is situated between Southampton and Fareham and boasts a huge fuel terminal, served via an undersea pipeline from a refinery on the opposite side of Southampton Water. During the Second World War a nearby aerodrome was used to train pilots of Spitfires, Lancasters and Wellingtons.

August

Left: **YORK** The Derwent Valley Light Railway was a privately owned standard-gauge railway in North Yorkshire and was unusual in that it was never nationalised, remaining as a private operation all its life. It ran between Layerthorpe on the outskirts of York to Cliffe Common near Selby. Between 1977 and 1979 the line's owner ran passenger steam trains between Layerthorpe and Dunnington – which is being approached by the train carrying Ray on 8 August. He snapped this picture from the footplate of the locomotive *Joem*, an ex-LNER Class 'J72' that is now preserved on the North Yorkshire Moors Railway.

In 1979 the passenger service ceased, but the railway continued to carry occasional freight trains to Dunnington until 27 September 1981, when the line closed. However, in 1993 a short section was reopened by volunteers, who now run steam and diesel services on Sundays and Bank Holidays. The line is nicknamed the 'Blackberry Line' because it used to transport blackberries to markets in Yorkshire and London.

Right: **RYDE** The next day, Ray and wife Joan were on the Isle of Wight, where Ray photographed the island's famous ex-London Transport tube trains operating at Ryde Esplanade station. That's Joan in the foreground, leaning against a lampost.

August

LEEDS On 12 August Ray was at Leeds station, where he couldn't resist getting 'Deltic' driver Ron Warren to pose at the cab of his mighty diesel after working No 55014 from London King's Cross.

ABERDEEN Ray's hectic round-Britain schedule continued on 28 August in Scotland. This is Class 26 No 26022 about to head the 11.50 train to Inverness.

EDINBURGH Ray is in Scotland to visit the Bo'ness & Kinneil Railway, the heritage line near Edinburgh. It is run by the Scottish Railway Preservation Society (SRPS), and today operates over 5 miles of track. Here an organist is trying out the organ in the ex-GNSR Royal Saloon on a Bo'ness Branch Special, organised by the SRPS on 29 August.

EDINBURGH Kinneil is a request stop on the line, and back in 1978 it was adjacent to a major colliery. Class 20 No 20011 is running round the SRPS special. Yes – yet another 'Chopper'!

September

Above: **READING** Yet more coal – this time empty wagons being hauled through Reading by Class 46 No 46009 on 7 September.

Right: **WIRKSWORTH** On 12 September Ray was in Derbyshire. His caption handwritten on the back of this photograph reads, 'Driver John Freeman (centre), known as The Godfather to his mates, with guard and second man at Wirksworth before leaving for St Mary's yard, Derby, with an afternoon limestone train.'

Far right: **DUFFIELD** The railway arrived in this sleepy Derbyshire hamlet in 1840, followed in 1910 by Rolls-Royce. It certainly wasn't sleepy on 12 September when Ray photographed two more 'Choppers' – Nos 20192 and 20172 – on the limestone train from Wirksworth.

September

Below: **WIRKSWORTH** At Wirksworth Quarry an 0-4-0 Baguley diesel is about to shunt a few wagons. The connection to BR's yard was via a short, sharply curved and very steep branch, which involved a reversal. Wagons were taken down a few at a time from the exchange siding at the top of the incline.

Right: **WIRKSWORTH** The 0-4-0 Baguley in more detail.

Below right: **WIRKSWORTH** It looks disused, but this is the end of the shunting neck on the short branch between the quarry and the exchange siding.

October

SINFIN It's 5 October and Ray is on a special excursion at Sinfin Central, south of Derby – appropriately enough formed of a Class 108 DMU built in the city. In fact, 333 of these versatile units were produced between 1958 and 1961, some remaining in service into the 1990s.

DERBY A highlight of the works tour was a Leyland bus-bodied railcar – note also the APT-P bodies being built in the background.

October

Below: **ABERNANT** Coal is a recurring theme of Ray's travels in 1978, and on 12 October he was in the Rhondda Valley in South Wales, at Abernant Colliery, where he spied this National Coal Board 0-6-0 shunter.

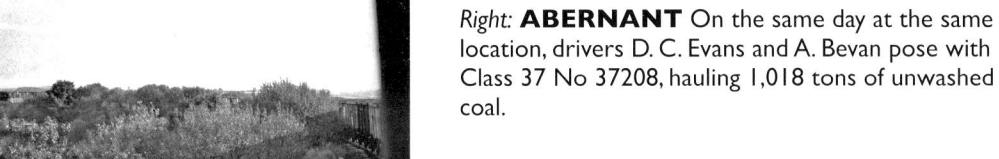

Right: **ABERNANT** On the same day at the same location, drivers D. C. Evans and A. Bevan pose with Class 37 No 37208, hauling 1,018 tons of unwashed coal.

Left: **ABERNANT** Ray hitched a ride in the brake van, from which he snapped this picture of the long train rounding a curve as it headed towards Swansea Docks. You can just see the Class 37 at the head of the train, on the viaduct.

Above: **MILFORD HAVEN** It's certainly a haven for shunters! Here are Fowler 0-4-0 *Charles Newbow* and 1954 Hudswell *Margaret Bristowe*, both owned by the Milford Haven Docks Board.

Above: **ABERNANT** Now Ray has swapped ends and, from the cab of No 37208, photographs the heavy train being banked up a 1 in 40 incline by another Class 37, No 37177.

Right: **MILFORD HAVEN** Still in Wales on 20 October, Ray photographed the Docks Board 0-4-0 Fowler shunter *P. J. Robjent*, with BR Class 37 No 37180 in the background.

November

FISHGUARD The driver of No 37179 is Owen Morgan, from Carmarthen.

FISHGUARD Back in Wales on 13 November, Class 37 No 37179 heads for the docks.

HERBRANDSTON Here's another Class 37, this time No 37176, hauling 55 empty tankers, plus brake van.

TORKSEY is famous for its viaduct, with two 130-foot steel spans across the River Trent.

TORKSEY On 11 November Ray photographed an RCTS rail tour at Torksey, in North Lincolnshire, with a Metro-Cammell DMU at its head.

December

PEMBREY On 20 December Ray rounded off his year with another trip to Wales. Today he's at Pembrey, Carmarthenshire, where he photographs a brace of Class 03 shunters that have just arrived from Cwm Mawr.

PEMBREY Looking back over 37 hoppers from the cab of No 03120, while No 03152 is at the other end, pushing.

COED BACH Ex-Southampton Docks shunter No 07006 stands by as No 03152 shunts at Coed Bach's National Coal Board washery.

1978 Happenings (5)

November (continued)
- Rioters sack the British Embassy in Tehran.

- Prince Andrew joins the Royal Navy.

- Pollyanna's nightclub in Birmingham is forced to lift its ban on black and Chinese revellers, after a one-year investigation by the Commission for Racial Equality concludes that its entry policy was racist.

- Viv Anderson becomes England's first black international footballer when he appears in a 1-0 friendly win over Czechoslovakia at Wembley.

- An industrial dispute closes down *The Times* newspaper for almost a year.

December
- Peter D. Mitchell wins the Nobel Prize for Chemistry.

- The Labour minority Government survives a vote of confidence.

- The Constitution of Spain is approved in a referendum, officially ending 40 years of military dictatorship.

COED BACH A better view of No 07006, one of two 07s at the NCB washery.

COED BACH No 03152 shunts a long train of washed empties.

CWM MAWR Nos 03120 and 03152 are now at Cwm Mawr Colliery yard, shunting.

December

CWM MAWR No 03152's driver Gwyn Morgan (Llanelli) poses with guard and second driver.

BICESTER A fine set of chimneys on display at Bicester on 23 December – inspiration for the modeller, perhaps? *Peter Butler collection*

1978 No 1 Records

January
Mull of Kintyre — Wings

February
Uptown Top Ranking — Althia and Donna
Figaro — Brotherhood of Man
Take a Chance on Me — Abba

March
Wuthering Heights — Kate Bush

April
Matchstalk Men and Matchstalk Cats and Dogs — Brian and Michael
Night Fever — Bee Gees

May
Rivers of Babylon — Boney M

June
You're The One That I Want — John Travolta and Olivia Newton-John

August
Three Times a Lady — Commodores

September
Dreadlock Holiday — 10CC
Summer Nights — John Travolta and Olivia Newton-John

November
Rat Trap — Boomtown Rats

December
Do Ya Think I'm Sexy — Rod Stewart
Mary's Boy Child — Boney M

Index

General
Advanced Passenger Train (APT) project 5, 21, 38
Bo'ness & Kinneil Railway 35
Derwent Valley Light Railway 34
Post Office Railway 9

Locations
Aberdeen 35
Abernant Colliery 39-40
Achnasheen 16
Armathwaite 1
Ashburys 11
Ayr 32
Bicester 47
Birkenhead 22
Brora 15
Brough 14-15
Clapham Junction 33
Clayton West colliery 7
Coed Bach Washery 44-45
Cwm Mawr Colliery 46-47
Dent 18
Derby Works 38
Duffield 36
Farringdon Street 10
Finsbury Park 14
Fishguard 41
Garsdale 17
Hamble 33
Heathrow Central 4-5
Helmsdale 16
Herbrandston 41
Hooton 21
Huddersfield 6-7
Ipswich 28
Kellingley Colliery 15
Killoch Colliery 32
King's Cross 13, 27
Kyle of Lochalsh 17
Leeds 35
Liverpool Street 28
Lymington 25-26
Marchwood 33
Milford Haven 40
Pembrey 43
Perth 17
Poole 22-24
Portsmouth 11
Reading 5-6, 19, 26, 36
Ryde 34
Sheffield 29
Sheffield 8
Sinfin 38
Stourbridge 30-31
Strome Ferry 16
Surbiton 8, 24
Tinsley Marshalling Yard 29
Torksey 42
Toton Sidings 29-30
Waterloo 12
Wick 16
Wimbledon 25
Wirksworth 36, 37
Worcester Shrub Hill 31
York 19-21, 34

Locomotives, diesel
Class 03 43, 44, 45, 46, 47
Class 07 44, 45
Class 20 29-31, 32, 35, 36
Class 26 15, 16, 17, 35
Class 31 14, 19, 28
Class 33 26
Class 37 20, 28, 39-40, 41
Class 40 11, 13, 19, 20, 21
Class 45 8, 19
Class 46 36
Class 47 6, 19, 24
Class 50 6
Class 55 'Deltic' 20, 35
Industrial shunters 16, 37, 40
NCB shunters 7, 39

Locomotives, electro-diesel
Class 73 12
Class 74 24

Locomotives, steam
LNER 'J72' *Joem* 34
LNER 'V2' *Green Arrow* 1, 17, 18
WD 0-6-0 *Waggoner* 33

Multiple units, diesel 6, 15, 33, 42
Class 108 38
InterCity 125 HST 5, 19, 26, 27

Multiple units, electric 13
Circle Line 10, 28
Class 418 12
Class 423 25, 26
Isle of Wight 34
Waterloo & City 25
Wirral & Mersey 22